Taking Up Our Daily Tools

Also by Al Maginnes:

Outside A Tattoo Booth

Taking Up Our Daily Tools

Al Maginnes

St. Andrews College Press
Laurinburg, North Carolina
1997

Thanks to Mike Chitwood, Rick Madigan, and the Black Socks Poetry Group for making specific suggestions that helped in the composition of these poems. And for their friendship and encouragement, my gratitude to LuAnn Keener, Suzanne Cleary, Michael Gills, Michael McFee, and Marty Silverthorne. And finally, special thanks to Joseph Bathanti.

Library of Congress Cataloging-in-Publication Data

Maginnes, Al 1957. Taking up our daily tools / Al Maginnes—
Laurinburg, NC / St. Andrews College Press
    I. Maginnes, Al. II. Title

St. Andrews College Press
1700 Dogwood Mile
Laurinburg, NC 28352

ISBN: 1-879934-51-5

First Printing: November 1997

Grateful thanks to the editors who first accepted these poems for publication in their journals:

Antioch Review: "My Father's Tattoo"
Georgia Review: "The Angels of Our Daily Bread," "Fairy
      Rings"
Countermeasures: "The Backyard"
Green Mountain Review: "The Sound of One Voice"
Independent (Durham, NC): "The Remembered World"
Indiana Review: "The Slow Hours"
Laurel Review: "Graveyard Bells," "The Music of Dust,"
      "Seasonal"
The Ledge: "Terminal Street"
Mid-American Review: "Annulment," "ConversationsWith Air,"
      "Practicing Magic," "Sharks In Kansas," "Sugar Lake,"
      "Wanderers"
Pittsburgh Quarterly: "Barga"
Poetry: "Harness," "Jobs"
Prairie Schooner: "Sealegs"
Quarterly West: "For The Players"
Shenandoah: "Capitulation"
Southern Humanities Review: "We Love What We Are .
      Formed By"
Southern Poetry Review: "Lake," "Salt, Fire, What Comes After"
Tampa Review: "Counting Toward Harmony"
Tar River Poetry: "Shearwaters," "The World Drowning"
Texas Review: "How We Listen"

"Jobs" was reprinted in *Family: A Celebration* edited by Margaret Campbell (Peterson's Press).

"My Father's Tattoo" appeared in the chapbook *Outside A Tattoo Booth* published by Nightshade Press.

"Conversations With Air" was reprinted in 1996-97.

For my mother and in memory of my father
And for Jamie, always

Contents

PART THREE

PART FOUR

PART ONE

Wanderers

In my version of "The Wanderer" by Dion
and the Belmonts, Dion hiccups one syllable
over and over while the tune vamps behind him,
postponing the final crescendo and silence.

If it does not happen that way, it should.
At the retirement home where my wife worked
for a short while, she was warned to keep an eye out
for "wanderers," patients who walked off

to pay a bill they received in 1956, to find
the husband or wife buried a decade before
and really give them the old what-for this time,
or to hail a cab back to the dance they left

laughing many years ago. Step by querulous step,
they seek to undo change, the single constant
time owns. And somewhere in the pasts they move toward
wait the bodies that could run, swim, make hard love,

hung now in some ghosted closet like a suit that
did not make the leap in style, giving no hint
of what bodies can fall to. No song in mid-romp
can know its ending. When "The Wanderer" strutted

from the radio of every parked car and every streetcorner
doo-wop boy wanted the note of tearing fabric
Dion's high notes held, did anything warn him
that he would find himself sick and out of heroin,

barely able to shuffle far enough down the street
to score? If he heard his songs then, on some passing
radio, were they mockery or did they lift him
into the nostalgic fog of those other wanderers

who live in the sweet hope of walking back in
while the music is still playing? On the dance shows
I watched on Saturday afternoons, the dancers always
moved for a long moment after the music died,

as if the body's suggestions were music enough.
And how many times have I stayed at some enterprise,
trying to succeed with repetition when strength
and inspiration failed? And sometimes that success has come.

Dion is clean now, makes the rounds of oldies shows,
singing his hits for men and women who listen
until the songs pare off enough years to make them
brash again. Shaking back the forward surge of years,

they take the floor. Sweating harder than distance runners,
they shuffle and turn toward the past music creates, a past
conversely more distant and more real, whose birthstone
is the silent music all wanderers make their own.

The World Drowning

Black water fills our basement,
underground cousin to the rain
that has run off our roof
for three days. The basement, big enough
for my sister and me to ride bikes in,
has turned swamp, lagoon, wild place,
one thin barrier holding it
from us. Anything unlucky enough
to be on a floor or low shelf
is gone. My father is down there,
measuring the water's rise, making
an inventory of what must be taken
to the curb for the city to haul off.
At the top of the basement stairs,
I count how many steps
the water has climbed, how many
before it eases under the basement door,
an oily wave trespassing
the kitchen's slick-polished tile.
Some afternoons I watch
a TV show, three guys took a raft
down a river and wound up
in prehistory. Like them
I understand all bets are off.
The skin that covers my life
could be torn back at any time
and the same black water
would force itself into the wound.
Stacking soaked boxes on his tool bench,
my father saves what he can.
I want to step down
into the new drowning room
so that I can be baptized in its danger

until the water, furrowed by any movement,
becomes just one more darkness
like the night I once feared
closing my eyes on.
I go to sleep hearing
water that falls to rise again.

Jobs

Tools had secrets
to make jobs get done:
claw hammer, power saw
I never had the skill to use.
My hands blistered to fit
shovel, rake, and hoe handles.
When I got a carpenter's bench
for my eighth birthday, it was my father
who built a bookcase, bird houses,
a wooden key with hooks to hang real keys on.
I watched, trying to discover
the life hidden inside tools.
He tucked his lower lip under his teeth,
hammered and measured his way
inside some concentration
I could not enter, my first glimpse
of the work men invent to answer
a bidding buried in the clank
and gearwork of the daily shuffle.
It would be a few years
before I walked onto a construction job
and learned men were identified
by the jobs they were paid for.
At the finish, they left their names
on I-beams, staircases, the backs of panels.
It was there my hands hardened
with the work underneath them,
and I learned the rhythm that progresses
to the long breath at the day's end.
I scratched my name
in the wet concrete of a grade beam.
In my first office job, the progress
of paper was endless. I signed nothing

to mark the work of my softening hands.
I wanted to build something
in my unpaid hours that would hold
solid and symmetrical as a right angle,
my name the only inessential thing.
My father never signed his bird houses,
but I have seen his name scribbled
over and over in the frantic work
of a young bird's wings
as it apprentices itself
to the job of flight

My Father's Tattoo

A bird of blue ink flew the inside
of my father's forearm.
Four inches higher, a patch of scar
marked a picture I never saw.
The missing tattoo may have marked him
deeper than the one that remained:
there was no story about either
told just after dark on the back porch
when the past seemed to glow
like the coals waning on the grill.

I see him in his Navy uniform
coming out of the dim parlor,
the sting in his arm forgotten
in an afternoon of beer and liberty.
He turns down the street with two friends
who will fade into cracked photographs,
a wife and family still remote
as mirrors of light
sun strikes from the ocean's rippled surface.

I used to believe the bird was real,
that it flew into my room while I slept
and my father watched.
Each night I planned to wake
and take its flight for myself.
During the years we had little to say
I stopped once outside a tattoo booth
on Carolina Beach's boardwalk
to scan the display of motorcycle wings,
mushrooms, skulls and slogans
for my father's bird. I moved off, wondering
if I could hold in my own arm
that piece of my father,
that throbbing flight.

Salt, Fire, What Comes After

It was salt I tasted when a bone-fisted boy
punched my lips into my teeth, the same
salt that Lot's wife became when she turned
to see over her shoulder the burning city
they fled. Three weeks earlier, I'd looked back
at Chicago's stained skyline and dirty snow
dissolving behind me, eroding like salt
as my father drove us to our new home in Georgia.
I'd seen a drawing of Lot and his daughters
fleeing into the desert, his wife behind them

frozen white by God's spare fury. I still wonder
why it was salt that she became. If the intention
was to hold her forever, why not granite?
Then we might still visit her where she stands,
monument to disobedience and impulse,
the tendons in her back-turned neck beginning
to crumble a bit, eyes stuck wide
from staring into that purge of flame.
Or why not sand, if no trace was meant
to remain? But perhaps the desire

was for something white, easily defiled,
illustration of the imperfect soul, the fate
of weak flesh. I once walked home
backward in new snow, delighted
that my footprints would mislead
any tracker. As we moved south,
I dreamed of being made new, graceful
as fresh snow. With no past,
I might be chosen for teams, be forgiven
my quick mouth and slow body. But we follow

ourselves wherever we go, our tracks
marring sooted snow and dry ground. Maybe
that's why I've always envied men and women
who disappear from their lives in mid-step,
not because of broken laws or creditors
but because some hidden limit was breached,
some flesh finally violated;
a stalled traffic light, a cashier's sneer,
and they clean out the bank account
and take a cab to the airport.

Sometimes they turn up years later,
tending bar in New Mexico, planting azaleas
in Dalton, Georgia. They just couldn't take anymore,
they say with the puzzled smile
of one having to explain something obvious
as gravity. They refuse to return, even
for a visit. They have learned the lessons
of Lot's wife and the penalties for looking back.
The real story is never so romantic, of course.
There are abandoned spouses, trashed promises,

the whole network of human grief.
We never mentioned Lot's grief in Sunday School.
Perhaps he simply refused the barter of tears
and the salt they paint across the face.
Now when I move, I seldom look back, too busy
loving the sense of flight, motion's power to save.
But two weeks after moving to Georgia, after walking
into a new classroom, my smart mouth got me punched.
The taste of my own blood swamped my mouth
as I fought back without power or passion

until someone of real size and ferocity,
tired of the show, separated us. Walking away,
flesh burning against the dry cold of a Southern winter,
I wanted only to disappear. Grateful

I was leaving no tracks, I looked back
as Lot's wife had, not at the fresh start
falling in flames behind me, but at what followed
and what lay ahead, waiting for another taste
of the salt-rich blood, the tears I bore
into this world I could not vanish from or flee.

The Music of Dust

The diamond-tough disc in my hand slurs
my face like a blues riff yet offers
a music so compressed and polished it reflects

none of the considerations of dust
and worn needles that stitched every syllable
of music I heard for years. Once I placed

one of the thick, one-sided platters my grandmother danced to
on a turntable. The strings and air-thin voice
were lost cries in the decades' valleys of gravelly dust

but enough gleamed through to understand
how that music must once have sounded,
the way my grandmother's face, in the forgiveness

of certain light, became the face of the girl
standing beside her new husband in photographs
she showed my sister and me before her body clouded

with the dust of years, reduced
to air and old songs. I know an old jazz player
who refuses to listen to compact discs.

"Too sterile," he wheezes, pulling on one of the cigarettes
that have taken his wind so far away
he can no longer blow his clarinet. The wind

that whispers in the horn's mouthpiece before its first cry,
the space between the horn and the drum is what he wants,
reminder of the human motors that toil

in the factory of melody. He handles his records

like jewels, the dust-free glide
of music over his speakers sustaining

his faith that reprieve from dust is possible.
No dust ticked the songs that played
through her mind's sound-proof chambers

in my grandmother's last years. Even distortion was kind.
And in memory's arrangements, those songs shone
more brightly than the glass-bead glisten

of piano notes that will spin from this disc,
weaving their false promise that music can rise
from the dust of this life and not return.

Barga

Now my mother opens
the cemetery's iron gate,
walks the rows of tilting stones.
She has no words to bless
in its native language this ground
where her grandfather lies.
The first from our side of the water
to see this place, she kneels
into her child's memory
of a brown-skinned man with quick fingers
for gardening and the mandolin,
who frowned at the edge of converstations
but whispered to her in a breath
that was Barga's black soil and olive blossoms.
He retired to Italy, left a buried wife,
a son married to America.
If the ocean was about to split
with blood and smoke and fire,
that was not an old man's concern.
His letters to America were news
of the weddings of cousins,
of weather and the vegetables
robbed from his garden by long-winged blackbirds.
Later there was no news at all.
The words of my mother's prayer are simple
but would puzzle a man
who never learned the trickery of English.
The past gets buried year by year
in church yards, fields, veteran's plots,
leaves us to reclaim what we can
from history's count, the awkward climb
to read the stone, the dirt that smears one knee.
In a graveyard in Barga,

one part of the growing past is delivered
from stone's blind erosion
by my mother's witness.
She says the carved name aloud
and feels the small giving of earth
beneath her knee.

What Fire Claims

I have tried to write this before.
After my grandmother died, leaving
her life as quietly as she inhabited it,
her body cremated. My mother was alone
when the funeral home delivered
the ashes, unsifted, in a plain cardboard box.
I thought of this last night as I cleaned
the wood stove. Charred wood knots, shined
by the fire that did not wholly claim them,
nestled deep in the bed of grainy ash.
Closer to the bottom of the stove,
I unburied a vein of breathing coals.
The air that lifted the feathery top dust
of ash in its swirl touched them
to an angry winking of fire. The box
was heavier than she expected, my mother said.
And she knew what rested in there
to lend it that grave weight:
chips of bone, teeth still loaded with silver
and saved from their final decay. We think
only a thin handful will remain,
a scattering to float on wind's halations
or dissolve in some patient water.
But holding that box, my mother knew
she would never cast those fragments
to any fickle air or gray ocean. She would bring them
instead to the ground, the only place
strong enough to bear what is left of us
after we have passed through fire.

The Backyard

Either prophecy or a desire to escape
the babysitter's gaze and her airless house drew me
        to that backyard, clotted by vegetation and vine,
by the rusted cast-offs of the thirty-five years residence
        of Mrs. Beavis, the obese woman who did not watch
my sister and me each Wednesday so much as she folded us
        into the myriad traffics of her family,
a multi-generational quilt of sisters and cousins,
        brothers and toothless nephews, all scarred,
all fascinated by the failures and afflictions of the body.
        They used the telephone to call doctors and taxicabs,
gummed the polysyllabics of their maladies
        into the oatmeal-thick air of Alabama summer
or lingered on aluminum porch furniture, "feeling poorly."
        And while they talked, I eased to the back of the house
to stare at the backyard, at the engineless, windowless car,
        the tumbled fence, the radius of damp dirt
around the cinder block steps that no spear of grass trespassed,
        where even the harshest sun, diffused by the leafy
cloud-reefs of a giant pecan tree, never stepped.
        Beyond stretched a tide of trampled yellow weeds,
rising here and there in the shape of whatever they covered
        like the nightmare shapes of roadside houses
and leaning barns swallowed by kudzu vine,
        forms rearing against the green plant's crawl,
the growth that can be measured daily can almost be watched
        by the unadorned eye. But here nothing grew.
Even the flowers seemed static, caught
        in the lassitudinal heat. And each time I started
to step into that unhealthy and enchanting quiet, Mrs. Beavis
        called,
        her voice reeling me back through the reek of collards
and Lemon Pledge, back onto the front porch where my

sister played
some wordless game and Mrs. Beavis and her visitors trod
a relentless litany of illness and I tried not to stare
    at the wounds, blossoms of decayed flesh, already
    displayed:
a one-eared man sipped iced tea all afternoon and never
    spoke a word,
    a woman, swollen by sugar diabetes, had to be helped
from her chair, a younger woman, legs slashed by deep
    purple scars,
    droned an entire afternoon about cancer's assault on her
    mother,
the first mention I'd heard of that restless disease.
    But this is about the single time we were taken into that
    backyard,
so Mrs. Beavis could direct three of her nephews
    as they cleaned up, the same way she directed
my sister and me in cleaning when she came to our house,
    pointing to the exact thing we were to pick up and the
    place
we were to put it. One nephew, probably no older than twenty,
    stood us near a catalpa tree, under the gaze of a leaning,
faceless scarecrow, guardian of a long-abandoned garden.
    Told not to move, we obeyed, not out of respect
but because the gaps between the nephew's blackened teeth
    were wells, pools we might fall into and never rise.
We stood among honeysuckle vine, Queen Ann's lace, rose of
    sharon,
    lush syllables the tongue drinks off as easily as it spins
tales of idyllic childhood without pausing over the fear of
    rusty nails,
    men without ears, diseases that swell and devour
the flesh. Fat bottleflies and tiny, feral yellowjackets
    orbited the rotting compost pile in drunken figure eights,
the smell rising like fever to advertise the decay that waits
    just under the sweet flowers of any life, even this one.
But when a thin vine of music wound across the fetid air,

I left my sister, walked toward the bent and toiling group,
the lopsided mound of trash they had assembled.
One of the nephews had uncovered a mud-caked,
reed-busted harmonica and now squalled from it
a rough mimicry of a tune. I moved closer
even as another nephew yelled for him to put that thing down
and do some work, even as my sister called me back,
even as Mrs. Beavis launched a dog's water dish, filled,
somehow, with motor oil, toward the trash pile. It hit me
instead, exploded a black star of oil across my chest.
Later, shirtless, I would follow two of the nephews
into the backyard, realm of broken tooth and jailhouse tattoo,
a life
I would spend years next to, never wholly joining or
leaving.
But I saw none of that coming as I tore open
the scarecrow's chest, featureless fabric and black straw
falling. Plunging in a hand to scoop out the straw, I touched
the damp heat of decay, felt the slow fires of our ruin, before
I yelled and jumped away, flapping my hands free of the
straw's funk.
Blind white worms wove the vegetable innards
of that effigy, final proof of the corruption that binds all flesh
and the ragged standards we raise in the likeness of flesh.

PART TWO

Conversations With Air

The pile driver on the building project
three blocks away shivers the air,
a noice as necessary and involuntary
as cries during love, as the noise
the deaf couple in the bookstore made
to tether the wanderings
of their hearing and incessantly talking son.
Soon that boy will learn
his parent's fluttering language of fingers,
his hands spelling out each one of his wants
as men on construction sites learn
hand signals to speak across the deafness
of too much noise. The wing-work of fingers,
of tongue, can say most of what we need
yet the pile driver's noise reminds me
that there is more to be said
than our language knows. In the recording
of Chet Baker's last concert, he pauses
at the end of each phrase of "All Blue,"
as if waiting for us to catch up
the way a parent might walk ahead
then turn and wait for a child.
And if that child, delighted at some music
the parent cannot hear, seizes his father's hand
and points to its source, what choice is there
but to smile, blessing that child's joy?
That must be what those sculptors
who discovered angels inside marble
tried to make eternal—the wordless goodness
man is capable of. Now we are silent
before those angels, listening
for the rustle of scaled wings, the conversations
with air that all flight, all language
finally is. Between blows of the chisel,
those scuptors listened and were answered.

The Angels of Our Daily Bread

Beside the imperfect cobble
of each task our tarnished
and clumsy hands turn to
rises the ghost of its conception,
built in imagination's pure moment
by the angels of our daily bread.
You see them in Renaissance paintings,
hanging over battles, famous births,
the claiming of new lands,
there to bless the work but helpless
to halt mistakes. See the worry
pinching their tiny eyes,
pouting their frightened lips
into empty kisses. Our realm
of bent nail and shaved door,
of the wired muffler and the slow leak,
must puzzle them. In their kingdom
doors do not stick. Clocks run.
Fountain pens hold their ink.
Flawless symphonies soar all day.
Some crafty hands seem to know that place
and bear down on every task
as if this chair or tire or sandwich
might be taken home by an angel.
I once worked for a carpenter
who drove each nail, made each measurement
with such steady accuracy
that I believed some impatient angel
must have whispered to him
of a place with no clumsy helpers,
or crooked boards or mistakes
in the plans. "I can make it work,"
he'd say, eyeing some tangle

my hands had made, and gather himself
around the task, an angel's incense breath
cooling the back of his neck.
I flexed chapped hands and watched
the job move one step closer
to the shadowless creation
that is the dream given us
each time we take up our daily tools.

We Love What We Are Formed By

Tail end of a day when summer
drought had choked the mud
to red powder. He watched me climb
out of the chest-high ditch, winked
to the foreman that I'd nearly earned
my money that day, a benediction
that made twilight silver and pure.
More than dollars or the girls
I wrestled on my sweaty mattress,
I desired the ease he lived inside.
There seemed to be nothing
his hard-knuckled hands could not solve
or had to do twice. I saw him build
a staircase, start a forklift
with a screwdriver, wire a hot switch
when no electrician could be found.
Ankle-deep in wet concrete, he'd bend,
gut swinging like a grain sack,
screed the mud to grade,
then sweep the float in arcs
gentle as wing-strokes, never lifting
his hand until all he could reach
was a glass-smooth field before him
Then he stepped back and bent to erase
the holes his feet had left, then back again
until the slab was poured and finished
and no trace of him remained.
Perhaps he is the one I look for
in the midden of dust-haze
over each job site. Who can tell me now
what each day's sweat is worth?
Who is left to bless what this day has earned?

The Desire of Tools

These hand tools, polished and arranged
on their flea market table, sell themselves
as antiques, collectibles though they might still
perform the tasks they were designed for.
This brass spirit level surprises the hands
with its weight and still balances
a true line, registers each tilt of the horizon.
I take up each tool, testing it as I did
in my apprentice days when I flirted
with trades like dance partners, never stopping
long enough to learn a single one.

The old men at the other end of the table,
their hands flat-knuckled monuments to work,
recall the hand plane gliding curls
the color of light from hand-milled boards,
recall raising a house, a barn
up from a notion into the world
of small adjustments designed to cover
the lack of a design. Behind their talk,
a paint-starved shed yawns its store
of still years into the vanishing afternoon.
Nails adjust their hold in the softening wood.

Corners slip out of square. The slow gravity
in old buildings becomes a tool
that undoes men's hands, pushing until sun slips
a chisel-blade of light through one seam.
Then one slow exhalation builds into another
until bones of light ladder their way across the floor
and the tools that make repairs decorate walls.
But the desire of tools is to be taken up once more,
partnered after long sleeping, like one asked
to dance after sitting idle for years, delighted
to find nearly-forgotten moves of use once more.

Sharks In Kansas

"Florida," she said. "Palentology." That afternoon,
May flattening into summer's long humid rows
might have remained where I'd buried it,

had I not read this morning
that the fossilized remains of a shark's jawbone,
fifteen million years old, were uncovered

in a Kansas riverbluff. I've heard that the weight
of air will crush the organs of sharks brought to land,
drown them in their own airless blood.

We cannot relax, become dangling bait
in the weightless element that sustains them.
Yet there are times gravity weighs down

our bodies as well. For two years, she
and I tracked each other's moves,
both of us in love with other people

and happy most days, but curious
about the quick flame of sun
on water we had seen in each other.

The single time we touched, she passed me a pen
and dry static ticked. Our hands flew apart,
afraid of being shocked, afraid of a time

electricity might not stop us. And tonight
I can imagine her taking my fleeing hand, saying
"Touch here," pressing my palm flat in the warm

dirt. "They used to swim down there,"
and, for a second, I'd swear I felt
one of those old hungry bodies, appetite

keener than instinct, passing below us
so deep we'd feel no ripple
until, half a continent beyond my imagination

of our bodies, the shark, mouth filled with food
and blood, would turn at the water's plankton-rich edge
to find the sea a dry shelf behind him and dive.

There are sharks, sharks in Kansas, still
swimming in water that has turned to stone,
bent in the memory of tides

to the exact angle I once saw her arm bend
across her lover's shoulder, the way
my wife put her arm around me

just as the theater darkened last night,
the way small boys hold to each other
before they become afraid of what touch can mean.

Maybe that fear never leaves us.
When she said "Florida. Paleontology,"
I did not move to wrap her in the thoughtless hug

I might have offered someone else, but said
"Arkansas" and "poetry." When she asked "So, when
will I see you again?" we both knew the answer.

We would remain finely separated
as bones in a skeleton, bound
but differing in every form and particular.

And if there was regret in our bone-thin smiles,
at least there was no blood on our lips
as we gave each other to the sweet
quiet afternoons of what might have been

and plunged into the currents that would bear
our cruising appetites afloat as we kept moving
to hold the land-bound weight
of our bodies from crushing us.

Lake

Because I learned to swim
in an ocean, the still surfaces of lakes
have always looked dangerous.
No fortunate tide waits there
to tumble one to shore;
algae and bacteria are free
to breed and bloom atop one another.

A body's natural impulse is motion.
There are always small tides
hammering away: blood, lungs, sleeping heart.
Lakes hold no response
to the thousand reflexes we call rhythm.

My sister and I wore tennis shoes
to shield our feet
from bottles and the jagged lips of rusty cans
the first time we stepped in a lake.
The water was warm as oil,
crowded with life the ocean kept
in the empty room of its bottom.

In high school, the furtive bonfires
that dotted the lake's edge
were its jewels, dancing rubies
we were drawn to, where we drank
and smoked until we were lifted
like the breeze-blown sparks
the fire snapped loose.
Sooner or later, someone mentioned
the girl who drowned out there
two or five or twelve years before.
The night I joined the other skinny dippers

in the black water, every floating
water weed that brushed my skin
was her finger, every cricket noise
or falling cry was her voice.

On the news tonight I watched
the search for two men
whose fishing boat overturned
on the same lake I knew from high school.
The camera followed two deputies
dragging a net. Over their shoulders
tilted the bank where I first heard
the name that kept me afloat then,
that will not swim back to me now.

She was at a party and walked
from the shrill circle of friends
to the thinnest reach of fire-glow,
the first lappings of blood-warm water.
Bride on the verge of two thresholds,
she must have stopped—
ring of fire? ring of water?—
before slipping quiet as a knife
into the lake's unmoving heart.

From the lake's center,
the bonfire was the flip of a matchstick.
The water was flat as a pan,
my head the only thing breaking
the star-polished surface.
It was the first time I feared drowning
though twice before I'd been pulled under
by current. Distant as sirens, the flames beckoned,
and I began the slow rolling back to shore.
I want to call my sister and ask her
across the waves of silence
if she ever heard that girl's name,

press the shell of the receiver
to my ear like one listening
for a tide long gone out
or a dredge's noise in bottom mud.

I should ask, too, if she remembers
the tendrils of buttery mud
snaking our ankles, how our feet sank
as step by step we walked in,
a self-baptism whose each move
trusted the bottom to hold.

How We Listen

I think I've figured out how
my wife falls asleep before the gray
bark and laugh of the TV but wakes
when I drop a spoon in the kitchen
or cough in the bathroom. Once
I saw a rock band that had hired
a string section to swell its sound.
When one violinist rose for a solo
the crowd grumbled into uneasy silence,
not sure what was required
but knowing a clenched fist cry of "Boogie"
would be an embarrassment, the same embarrassment
that settled across the violinist's face
when he sawed and jabbed at the encore
of "Johnny B. Goode." Yet I swore
I could hear his instrument leaking
through the weave of drums and guitars
the way my wife hears, even in sleep,
the tiny anomalies that puncture
those brawling pageantries of sound
that curtain one end of the house.

It's the voice's flutter, the tickle,
like the hair of light hissing
between the drapes that leans our listening
in a new direction. I still hear
how the air in the restaurant shifted
when the woman at the table next to mine
began crying. She ordered the lunch special—
fried catfish, hush puppies, french fries, slaw—
before her face folded into ruin
and she sobbed into the folded dish of her hands.
The noontime tide of talk slowed.

Forks chimed against plates.
Quick gossipy whispers swallowed words.
I turned the page of my newspaper
soft as a leaf, trying to hear
in the rush of hushed voices
around me the source of her grief.
The waitress set a stack of extra napkins
next to the woman's tea and butter.

We turned away from her and the song
her sobs let us hear too clearly, back
into the lower-pitched business of our lives
the way the violinist must have listened
through the amplified rhythms
to hear shreds of simple finger
exercises he had once practiced.
My great-aunt swore once
that she could hear my sister and me
over all the other voices
galloping across the playground.
I was sure then she exaggerated
to reprimand our carrying on,
but now I believe her, believe
that some voices, some sounds are lifted
to us so that what we hear
is a sketch, a selection
of details continuous in their arrivals.

Once during a Christmas ice storm,
my great-aunt and her sister, my grandmother,
called. While I thanked them
for the book and the sweater
and answered questions about school,
both of them on the line, both
talking at once, the weight of the ice
broke a connection somewhere,
sealed the line so that I could hear

their voices but my words would not carry.
I heard them question each other,
then trickle to silence, each of us
suddenly filled with the weight
of all that needed to be said
now that no one could hear.

The Sound of One Voice

When I'm talking dinner plans and basketball
with my friend over the phone, his wife
is behind him calling him to remind my wife
or me to bring the book she asked for
while my wife asks if they want us to make
salad or dessert. Our conversations go
like that: an orchestra tuning,
farting horns and tightening strings
working up to something melodious and important
we will eventually say
to a room full of waiting ears,
pink edges tilted like teacups
to the dancing flute of our words.
We have so much to tell, it boils
out of us, spills in the lap
of the bank clerk, the cab driver,
the woman with the clown-red hair
who wedges her cart in front of ours
in the checkout line. Sometimes,
when a band is in high gear,
I try to pick out one instrument—
lead guitar, bass—to find the place
it holds in the conversation
before it slips into the gap
between strike and sound
where music unwinds into memory.
Our own voices raise to an amnesiac blur
that dissolves any single word
the way sound is swallowed in outer space.
I saw a ticker tape parade for some astronauts
on TV once. I remember
the uncertain smile of one as he and his friends
waved into the vacuum roar of hungry throats.

Thousands of shredded newspapers,
millions of words, stormed around his ears,
a far cry from the one voice
lasered to him from Houston
to relay weather, box scores,
soap opera plots, good luck telegrams.
I know that music is pumped into space
and it's easy to imagine
that astronaut's hearing narrowed
to pick out the same thing I would
in, say, a Motown tone: a guitar
thin as a bee's stinger, riffing
between gospel voices and chewy bass.
The next day, brooms whispered
spaghetti-tangles of paper into piles,
word on top of chopped word,
chronicle of our every move
across this blue stone that is
always half-shadow, half-light.
The astronaut woke up humming
that guitar-dance deep in his throat,
the buzz beneath his gravity-thick tongue
holding him, note by half-note, from passing
the one voice he owns
into the confetti of human speech.

Sealegs

The two pelicans flying parallel
to the ferry from Hatteras to Ocracoke
must have been joined by something
finer than wire or the one in back

could not have mirrored the leader's
belly-skim and rise so exactly.
I watched until the deck's pitching
as we crossed another ferry's wake

tossed me into how often
another person's passage throws us off balance.
Once I watched a girl in a jewelry store
dump a display rack of gold chains into her purse.

I waited for her outside, unable to believe
what we'd gotten away with.
Before the hand on my shoulder.
Before the accusations and lies. The tears.

All day memory has been a bad navigator,
steering me over and over to the sandy
burials of old disappointments and loss,
one more sight for the tourists

crowding the bow of the boat that cruises
the point, showing off old landmarks.
There is the Wreck of the Jilted Chump.
Over here is the Bay of Bad Dancers.

The fishermen who work this water
divide the ocean's field of chop and slough
into smaller territories, the way we invent
names for who we are or used to be.

Feel the fine chain's hook between your fingers.
The shine is what lures us.
The pelicans flew beside us a while,
then curved back as precisely

as if they followed a treasure map's pacing
to the X marks the spot of hidden loot
that every coastline claims to harbor,
that we believe in like a horizon's promise

even though it's heavy, a risk to acquire
and the first thing we'd shed
to swim. Or fly if that were all
that anchored us to this ground

the fishermen tie themselves to
when the sun has dropped to a red weld
sealing the flat plates of water and sky.
They weigh the fish they plundered the ocean for,

hoist the heaviest ones for mug shots
while the ones that slipped the hook
swim forgotten under sea
that still flashes and wobbles in their legs

as they spread the shaky wings of the day's legend
into the first clanking flight of a seabird.

Harness

The dog whines for food and a walk,
turns three circles to scare off snakes
before he flops on the kitchen floor.
Once, his ancestors came,

all dripping chops and shaking haunches,
to the smell of the meat whose hiss and sizzle
blacked the air outside the unsteady glow
cast by man's just-tamed fire.

The first dog nosing into the light
toward a fat-mottled bone
could not see the leash waiting to tug him
toward the sit-stay of bred habit

any more than the first man
to touch a living animal could feel
the fields turning, the cities rising
in the wing of muscle under his hand.

Even as we sewed their harnesses,
we've wanted what we took from them.
That's why we've invented machines
that fly, that run and swim faster

than we can muster, and one reason
we've always hunted the animals
that turned from the fire,
their tails a flame-bright flicker

disappearing in the shrinking dark.

Shearwaters

Some have been found broken on shore,
brown rags, grounded at last.
The myth of these birds says
they never make land, but spend
their lives in sea-flight, riding the tides
of trade winds, fed by what is lifted
to the water's surface. And perhaps wind
renders nourishment enough,
lending its muscle to the motion
of wings, the hammering that fastens
brassy sidings of light to each glassy wave.
But each day's labor is undone
by the shift change in the surly heavens,
leaving only stars to be swallowed
in rills and striations of water, irretrievable,
like nails driven too deep in soft wood.
Dawn might give the most hope,
the black ocean suddenly fire,
enticing one too rash to refuse
to dip its wings in the glowing.
This is how enchantment betrays:
oil gums the feathers or they tangle
in the empty lung of some torn
and discarded net, heaving now
with its final and unexpected catch.
But the one that refuses the offering
of the fiery water rises over
the burn-off of surface mist,
its wings horizon-lit sails
a marooned sailor might see,
might for a flutter of breath
believe to be an angel bearing down,
scarlet with deliverance's false light.

PART THREE

Human Sentences

By now the tale of the elephant
hung in Tennessee in 1916
for trampling her trainer to death

has been written so many times
it has become a kind of shorthand
for Southern gothic or the limits of jurisprudence,

some guilty gray mass heaved up
to choke on its own weight.
I thought of her futile death as I made

notes on the capital punishment reading
I had assigned. In a time when all souls
were judged wicked beyond redemption,

animals, even cockroaches, were tried
and sentenced to state execution.
It makes a scene the imagination loves:

the black-hooded ax man warming up
his hefty arms, cleaving the air
with practice cuts. The condemned dog wags,

pleased to be in the middle of so much attention,
licking his chops perhaps, after a last meal
of meat scraps and water. When sturdy hands

lower his head to the chopping block,
the dog stops wagging, looks doubtful.
Last week while I read, the phone rang

and a voice whose face I had not seen

in years told me that one more someone I knew
had died—by his own hand this time,

found hanging in the basement of a house
where he had rented a room. I hadn't known him
beyond a handful of facts—just someone else

in a town full of souls on their way
somewhere else. He stirred chili and flipped burgers
in a place I sometimes ate, drank

in the same bars, turned up at the same parties.
For tomorrow's discussion, I will tell my class
that the last time a man was hanged

in this country, a boy in Italy watched
a report on that execution and hung himself
four days later. I have some witty things

to say about government execution of cockroaches,
but too much wit might rob the air—some events need
to breathe their own ironies.

The elephant was not hung
in the conventional sense, but hauled,
in an awful feat of engineering,

by inches into her own death, pulled upright
by winches and logging chains
that strained until her back feet

left the ground so she could lawfully strangle.
He left a note saying who should get his dog
and that the money in the dresser should pay

for food and shots. There was no reason,
he said, for her to be put to sleep. No reason
for this animal to receive a human sentence.

46

Improvising Faith

Because I have not been to the churches
where spirit lifts worshippers,
turns their voices to sudden living
nerves, reeds vibrant with wordless melody,

I have only heard that such improvisations
of witness might last minutes or hours
before they subside and leave the speaker,
a spent instrument, breathless

and for a time, not quite at home in the body.
On Sunday mornings, Mike listens to Bill Evans,
the only music he can be so lost in
he forgets the years of Sundays

in those bare and tiny churches. Fifteen years
and still his family hangs up when he calls.
I told him once about a neighbor who blasted
the Sex Pistols out his window on Sunday mornings.

Mike smiled. "We all need our hymns."
Five nights a week, he plays piano
in hotel bars and steak house lounges.
He doesn't sing, tries to ignore

requests for "Summertime" and "The Way We Were"
from wet-eyed drunks who stuff dollars
in his fishbowl-sized brandy snifter and never
notice when he vamps into "Thirty Four Skidoo."

I used to listen to some jazz cuts
over and over, trying to find the cornerstones
of music that flees from, plays hide-and-seek with
written melody. Too long memorizing

the piths and gusts of those tunes,
and I apprehended every sliding note
but had no room left for improvisation's work.
The faithful never rise

to their ecstasy anywhere
but in church—husbands do not lapse
in glossolia over car engines or find prayer
guttering out of raptured wives whose hands

swim in dish water. Like the jazz players,
they need a place to depart from and return.
Mike departed long ago but says he understands
the raptures that let some believers take up snakes.

Faith that does not risk something is not faith.
One night as he played, a man at a table
cut his hand with a broken wine glass
and hurled blood on the woman

beside him. His voice rose to a wordless blur
as the waiters wrestled him out the door.
I wanted to know what happened next.
"I got to play the tunes I wanted all night," Mike said.

This morning, the father who will not speak
his only son's name rises, swaying
like a serpent charmed by eerie music
and the glissade of prayer fountains,

holy improvisation, through him again.
When blood was gathering in the cup of that man's hand,
Mike said, his face was the face of man so taken by spirit
he had no idea what his next word would be.

Counting Toward Harmony

Some minutes exist whole inside themselves:
times we meet our own eyes in a mirror
or slip between the recited notes
of an old song or bend into the last bars
of the solo, when blood's gravity meshes us
into the workings of a greater pulse. Grade
by slow grade, the notion of something just past
the visible has hammered in me a hope

that some hidden network of gear
and counterweight strives to bring
a long balance to our lives. I trust
the pendulum to swing as far east as west,
a steady measure of the heartwork of gears
that turns the world's rusty locks. This faith
lets me believe the hands of the clock
as a musician trusts the time his hands find.

Sometimes when a jazz drummer
pauses in his inventions and I hear
the unhurried tick of the high hat
beneath the hot and honey blue
of the melody, I am sure
our lives accumulate meaning
the way songs point without
strain to the final note,

but the zero of the clock face mocks us
with its refusal to add up to more
than the push of minutes that each hour
gathers its two hands as if in prayer.
The slap of two hands is our first counting
of the ticks we will never know the sum of,

that unwind our lives even as we push
to keep our ragged time.

Perhaps this is our trick: to love
the time that counts past our ability
to fathom when our hands fall still
as a tired drummer's after the clock winds
around to last call. The band puts down
instruments for cigarettes, water-weak drinks.
One couple still turns in the center
of the floor, their time reflected

in measures no music is written for.

The Remembered World

Perhaps only memory provides the whole picture.
I'm glad I don't have to go back there
to see the rusty chain stretched across the vacant dust
of the road to the closed down drive-in.
I'm glad I don't have to see the yellow weeds
coming up through the venous cracks
in the thin concrete apron, the hieroglyphs
of rust on the mute speaker poles,
the screen that has lost enough panels that something
essential would disappear from every scene.
I'm glad I wasn't there to trace the slow curve
of decline from two-dollar triple features to porno
to Saturday morning swap meets, all the barter
of what had already been refused. I'm glad
that what I know of that place is the warm
Friday nights my parents pajamaed my sister and me,
put us in back of the station wagon where we fell asleep
after popcorn and cartoons. Every week I dreaded
and waited for one preview: a shot of a man
sentenced to be buried alive. The camera stayed
tight on the face that showed through a window in the coffin
as the man was carried to his waiting grave. Every week
I fell asleep looking up through the curved glass
of the station wagon's back window, faint stars
and moon lost in the glow of the screen,
the car safe with the distant sounds
of a world I didn't remember but wanted to.
Years later, I would have a neighbor whose television
was a world of late-night intrusions, playing just feet
from where my head rested against our shared wall.
His laughter, the sound of a man living alone
and unused to laughing, boiled through the walls
as I lay awake, buried under his delight

in TV's rabble of voices. Sometimes on the foggy edge
of sleep, I'd hear his voice talking into the phone,
one more noise to furnish his small hours.
One day my phone rang and the IRS was on the line
asking for my neighbor, the first time
I'd heard his name. Had I seen him? Well,
could I walk next door and knock or leave a note?
No, they couldn't tell me how they'd gotten my number.
A few days later, that neighbor was gone, his rooms
silent, his windows suddenly empty as the screen
of that crumbling drive-in. I don't know anyone
who's ever seen that movie or even the single scene
of that man staring up from his own coffin,
drums marching in the background, but my neighbor
might have understood how that face furrowed
in its futile tally of old debts, might have understood
what it was to be buried with no choices in the middle of a life,
the view through the glass screen precious as escape
as he was borne out of the remembered world.

The Slow Hours

His best times the summer he was eighteen
were the afternoons when, between getting off work
and dark, he got in his car alone

and did not drive to his parents' house
and the slow angers that made a home there
or to find one of the endlessly tan girls

always just beyond his reach or the friends
poised like him on some uncertain brink,
high school too close to forget, the future

a vague looming payment to be met.
Instead he drove the country roads at a crawl,
following the settle of light on tobacco fields

and wide acres of hay as the sun commenced
its long falling from the dusty sky.
Sometimes he would end up by the brown lake

north of town. If no one else was there
he'd park and bury his bare feet
in the silt and fine dirt that passed for sand.

One afternoon he sat out there until full dark
and while the crickets barked up the fresh moon
that made a cathedral of the ground,

the scrubby trees and dingy water,
a pang somewhere resolution and prayer
whispered that his life might slow

to something he could take hold of and turn

like the driving wheel of his old Chevy.
There would be no backseat rider yelling for speed,

no one to tell him to get up for the job he hated
so he could be on time to lie down for the endless shit
adulthood seemed designed to carry

into dumb shades of death.
It would be fine to say that his life changed
that afternoon, that he gave up

the blurred nights of beer or the speed-laced
acid whose mindless, teeth-grinding rush
seemed the chemical distillation of all

his life had pared itself to. But he did not.
It was years and miles in another direction
before he remembered how slowly

he pulled away from the lake,
the radio switched off so he could savor
the quiet crunch of tires on the gravel road,

the cycle hum of crickets, the onion glow
of his headlights opening into the idea
that all this forward motion might lead somewhere.

Sometimes on those slow drives, he played a game,
turning off one county blacktop onto another,
not worrying about direction

or where he would end up, just trying
to keep going to avoid any intersection
or crossroad, any sign that would tell him to stop.

Fairy Rings

Neither the wedding waltz
of dust-starred mites
nor the old buck and wing
of cloven hoof dances
the brown rings into the grass,
but the teenage mother dangles
those bedtime enchantments
before the sleepy child
to keep him from the scarier truth:
the slow grind of fungus
that chews to wet stink and splinter
the tree stumps buried
by landscape and back fill,
the hidden use earth has
for what is trusted to its care.
Now the rot works up
as tree roots once worked down
and the old tales are dusted off
for dancing one round more
in flimsy shawls of leaf mold and wind,
for who among us would not wake
in the dankest, crumble-hearted
night hour to witness
the fairies' circling ballet, blessing
from a world so close to our own
we find the tracks its tenants make
leaving a mother's mouth,
the one place
science and magic lie together.

Seasonal

Three weeks after we carried out the wood stove,
ashy iron relic of winter,
spring is dropping into summer's ferment,
a visible motion beneath the day's greening.
Still, when a stray breeze gets carried
down the chimney's gullet, a breath
of winter's soot and old ash fills the room.
This morning after I dumped food scraps
and the wood stove's last ashes
onto the compost pile to be cooked again
in that flameless heat, I leafed
the newspaper's gray pages to learn
that someone I knew from high school
was caught burning two bodies,
presumed to be his wife's and a missing neighbor's
The stories flared out from that single fuse of fact
like the iris that spreads its papery petals
briefly and spectacularly each May:
interviews, profiles, and photographs
all shake down to no one knows why
he did it and the remains are still anonymous.
Last spring when we turned up our garden, we found
beer cans, a plastic shoe, both halves
of a shirt torn in two, other things
we couldn't name that had not been wholly claimed
by earth's crawling fire.

He never went to class. I'm trying
to reconcile the mug shot in the morning news
with my memory of a lank-haired boy
slouched behind the wheel of a muscled-up Nova.
His car's dark-throated rumble blosssomed
over the parking lot each morning

as he cruised through to pass joints
and see if anyone was up for a day off.
I never rode with him.
He went to prison the year I started college.
I thought I saw him once, chopping weeds
with a prison gang beside the highway.
Last fall I tore ashy stalks
of tomato plants from the soil, pulled up
the stakes, broke the brittle rags
that tied them upright. Today, I'll plant new ones.
The news of the smoking bodies will bloom
like some thorned and poisonous flower
that lives a few days before being uprooted
by some new malevolence whose name none of us knows.
Sometimes with my hands rooted in dirt,
I forget that I'm raising these plants to die.
I don't know how we become the people we are.

Creed For A Black Thumb

Lord, bless and accept the weeds
    I have not pulled from your gardens,

forgive the bare tomato vine,
    the fruit I did not harvest.

Forgive the drought I have imposed
    on all my gardens which are your gardens

and are bare.

      Pray, do not neglect me
as I have neglected them. Recall instead

    the hour of earth's breaking, the dull
blades of mattock and shovel

    rising in glory and falling in sweat. Recall
the eyelid of darkness that closed

    on handfuls of fruit, arms loaded
with flowers that serve no one

    but release pollen and perfume
in clouds as fine and as temporary

    as prayer.

PART FOUR

Annulment

I know the webbing of scar across her face
still keeps her from mirrors, the woman
I handed a towel to on the black crossroads.
Her wordless sobs, her husband moaning,
"Honey, honey," still slow me some nights

when I'm lost and pressing too hard
down a strange road. My three friends and I topped
the hill in time to see a truck's headlights dip
off the road, the car it had hit swinging to a stop,
hood gaping over the crumpled front end.

Radiator steam plumed like a distress signal,
dyed red in the ruby panic of brake lights.
We were 18. Our lives were a movie.
And now, memory like a camera performs
its dispassionate algebra of image and angle,

the fleshy confusion of what happened
dissolved to something as artful and distant
as the tiny, untouchable battles
on the evening news. The windshield sagged
under the curve of the night's sudden weight,

a hole punched in its center.
She was standing in front of the car,
crying for her ruined face, her husband helpless
beside her. I could roll a joint
or peg a mailbox with a bottle,

but this froze my hands as my mother's hands
must have frozen in gray dishwater
when the olive Army sedan pulled dusk up our street.

She watched with every other parent
to see which house it stopped in front of.

The towel I brought from the back seat
was a small flag waving truce
for all I could not do.
It was too dark to see the woman's face.
Something splashed on the pavement.

Another set of headlights flared over the hill,
and like a deer frozen in the shock of light,
we turned our bright, startled eyes to meet it.
The pickup's driver reeled up, whiskey-reek
rolling off him like a cloud.

Suddenly the intersection swelled with braking cars.
Someone yelled something about phone calls
and the rescue squad. Doors slammed. Voices rose.
I couldn't see in the windows of the olive sedan
or understand why my mother called me home.

From the edge of my yard, I watched the grim,
uniformed men get in their car. Their headlights unrolled
a thin carpet for them to glide away on.
Dark wrapped the street like a cocoon.
"Let's get out of here," our driver urged,

and we remembered the pot in our pockets,
the beer and speed in the car, the party
we had been looking for. We were 18.
We could change nothing. So drove away.
And may drive still, disappearing

into the gravity-rich dark that collapsed
into the hole at the center
of the maze of dying stars
that the windshield had become, an impossible

tracery of lines I still get lost in

each time I tell this story.
I watched a man die outside a bar once
and have never forgotten
the way his face blanked, veins
darkening into the numbered roads

of maps, each one winding nowhere I wanted to follow.
The news stayed off the night the olive sedan left.
And if a veil of scar still marries the woman
to that night, only in this version
of the story do I become the rogue groom

who flees the sheets of the marriage bed
as they stain with their announcement
of what was saved and what was not,
who hopes the night closing behind him
will heal any broken thing.

Sugar Lake

I know people forget the names
of old lovers. I cannot forget one.
The name I can't rescue this afternoon
is spray-painted across a sheer granite wall
at Sugar Lake, the name of the boy
who dove from the quarry's gnarled stone lip
into the embrace of the reflection
that rose from the black depths
to take him under. Weeks after that drowning,
I went there with a girl I thought I loved.
All afternoon those letters stared at us,
tribute to the existence of one
so dedicated to memory he lowered himself
over the wall's edge or rose,
hand-grip by finger-hold, from the water
until he found a place to perch
while he wrote that name.
The names of the dead are our prayers, proof
that we have not fallen. She and I fell
into the reflections of ourselves we buried
in each other and rose, our names empty
as water in the other's mouth. Swimming was banned
at that quarry when summer ended.
But last night, as you and I parked at a restaurant,
we heard someone else had drowned
in that water, one of the unnamed
night swimmers who flow over the rusty fence
for the long fall between stone and water.
If they saw that name at all, a scar faded by now
into the grain of rock, it was as faint
as the swift, thin clouds that gauze the moon
and vanish, the way our names unravel
into the exhalations of years. After we die,

our names will be everywhere for a time:
in the steam rising from a coffee cup,
waiting on corners for buses that don't come,
gathered in the space between a friend's inhale
and long sigh. Then we are smoke, lost
to all but a few. In the restaurant's kitchen,
white-aproned cooks moved in diaphanous steam,
sweating angels, nameless in the bodies of clouds.
I reached for my water glass but caught your hand,
you whose name I will not forget
and need not say. Maybe touch is all
that lets us forget that long falling
from which we will not rise, that will leave
only our names for friends to call,
to echo off granite walls and climb,
spare handfuls of letters sprayed across
the empty slates of black water.

Terminal Street

I never meant to leave there or come back
for fear I'd meet myself on the paint-starved porch
of one of the unnumbered houses just past

the spot where the stained sidewalk buckles
and thins to a crumble of gravel and black dirt.
That life was always we. Always waiting.

Groups swirled on porches, huddled in living rooms
to pass joints and dishwasher epiphanies
hand to hand while we watched for our lives

to pull up gleaming at the curb.
Someone new was always crashed on the couch.
Someone else was always moving out,

a chair, a mattress, a pillowcase of clothes.
The drugs we took did not let us sleep
or forget the university three blocks away

that most of us had come to town for
only to escape its towers of windows that would not open
into jobs we worked just enough

to pay for real life: pounding light of bars,
rooms crowded with strangers and smoke,
the sacrament of lined mirrors, all of us

bent in our rush to forget where
we arrived from, how we got here.
Say it: we were in love with our poverty.

When we threw the furniture we salvaged from curbs

into our bare front yards, it was proclamation:
we needed nothing. Not the littered rooms we lived in,

the jobs we changed like socks, the paychecks
we could not wait to blow.
Nothing comes as cheap as memory's high.

A girl whose parents waited in the car
while she gathered her albums,
kissed everyone goodbye, taped her new address

in Vermont or Colorado to the refrigerator.
She stopped, eyes blurred and shining, to say
"God, I already miss this place," and she was gone.

Each morning the water stain on my ceiling
made the shape of a new continent.
After every rain, plaster gobs smeared the stairs.

The black dress girls who work in bars,
the boys with the names of their bands
tattooed on their skinny arms

can't cure nostalgia's hangover and don't want to.
They don't want to hear that they'll ever
want to move away. And I'd never tell them

that a part of me I love
still waits on that street, still waits
to score, to catch the smooth ride,

to let the man I have become come back
to explain how and why he left here
and where he found worth going.

The History of Plumbing

Because all summer our unpredictable pipes
have refused to let sinks empty, soapy pools turning gray
then suddenly gone, toilets brimming dangerously full

before the coughing flush, because no chemical solvent
or probing tool has eked out the problem, because this
is the last step before calling a plumber I can't afford,

I crawl at last under the house to sound the maze
of cast iron, copper, and plastic, a twentieth century plumbing
history, that daily delivers and disposes of

such water as our unthinking needs require.
Somewhere above me, in the skeleton of floor joist,
ductwork, pipe and wire, lives every secret of this house,

switches that set no light burning, floorboards
that sigh as they shift in a tuneless echo of weather and gravity.
Because I worked on new buildings that rose slick

as glass out of the mud, square and tight around the secret
core of light and silence that all buildings fight
to keep in, I thought I had the skills I needed

to solve the slow fractures of an aging house.
When the last workers ride the clock, dallying
over the final items on the punch list,

each room brash with the smell of new paint,
lumined so brightly the light seems to live
in the body of the room, it seems impossible

that those whispering doors tick and whine,

for pipes to shudder and moan under floors, for life-line cracks
to crawl down walls until a new crew is called in

to fix what can be rescued. Our fathers didn't call
plumbers or repairmen; they took the tools
their fathers had left them and worked

straight to the heart of what needed fixing.
A friend told me that his father had broken
his hip, could no longer shovel his walk or grow

corpulent tomatoes and peppers.
Like me, he spent Saturday mornings
handing tools to his old man, nodding like he understood

his father's explanations.
Like me, he never believed these were problems
he would be called on to solve. Lying on my back,

I can almost see beyond cloudy insulation
and tired floorboards, through plaster ceilings
and the boxes of air they rest on,

through the roof's peeling shingles into rooms
I have not entered yet. The damp ground is ripe
with what has been left unlearned and unburied.

I tap this pipe, then that one, trying to hear through
the hollow notes to the problem I haven't solved.
I still have some of my father's tools,

shelved and hidden in a box, waiting for my hands
to grasp enough history to make a sluggish pipe run clear,
one more instruction my father can't call back

from the room where he waits. He once took us
to a Homes Of The Future exhibit; in the center

of a hall of sleek, humming appliances, a film unreeled

a future of dustless rooms, foil-wrapped gourmet meals,
families whose only job was harmony.
The machines would be perfect so we would be perfect as well.

I would not stain my white shirt with ketchup,
the heel of my sister's shoe would not come unglued,
we would not get lost and drive

blind loops for an hour, searching the way
to our rattling, leaking, present-tense of a home
whose very silence as we entered echoes now

to remind me that what we inherit
takes all our skill to repair
and all our love to pass on.

Capitulation

We're settling for too little,
my friends and I, rooting
in our small gardens, our bets
precisely hedged. One friend stays
couched in his living room,
grays the air with cigarette smoke,
bordered by the arching ball
of whatever sport's in season
and the weekly poker game.
The one who quit smoking
no longer writes, as if language too
were something to be dragged in
and slowly exhaled. It must be
a slow thing, this desire
to play with no wild cards,
to count your drinks and go home early.
A bartender we knew let us
borrow money to keep drinking.
We lived in a house rent-free,
dragged home branches and two by fours
to stoke the sheetmetal stove.
But we never mention the windy night
we lay on the steep-pitched roof,
our feet braced against gravity,
and believed the dusty,
impossible fire of stars
might even melt dawn's cold erasing.
Maybe we learned for good that night
not to desire more than we could touch.
If the Lord's Prayer can be lasered
onto a mote of dust eleven times,
what faith cannot dwindle
to turn our eyes from stars

to dirt? Maybe the quality
we have named vision requires
a kind of sustaining blindness,
a disregard for the rusty nails
and roots lurking to tangle
our feet. We stood on the roof
and stretched in the first utter light,
stunned by the sudden way
height flattened to mere distance,
disappointed by all we could see.

Practicing Magic

In the bar where the old men
of the neighborhood drink, the TV stays on
all day and no one pays any mind
to the young, frenetic lives splashed there.
When those men speak, they commence
mid-story, knowing their listeners can
provide context. More often, they are silent,
multitudes of lives suffocating
behind their clamped lips. When I drank,
I believed in proximity, spewed
explanation and confusion until all
my tricks lay bare. One afternoon,
the most silent of the old men
showed me the three-card molly, the first time
I'd seen it done. His hands,
gone to stone with arthritis and booze,
trembled over the cards, and I almost felt cruel
when I pointed to the red card.
He turned it over. Black.
I never found it once. When I asked
the secret, he looked at me
a long time and said I had to hold
my mouth right. Seven dry years
have made my mouth speechless as dust,
my compromise with the mysteries
of hand and eye and the distances they work in.
But distance demands narration
or at least the distraction
the carpet of TV noise provides
while we practice the trick
of our lives in mirrors,
hoping to get it down so well
method evaporates into pure result,
a secret we could not explain
even if we were sure of it.

Graveyard Bells

In a century when spirits
treated seances to trumpet serenades
and called the names of loved ones
from inside walls, one medium buried
his assistants alive with tubes to breathe through
and to speak into, to answer qustions
for the audiences gathered to hear the voices
of the dead. When the performance was ended,
the medium sealed the tube. The next day,
a body was removed. In New Orleans
when bodies were not embalmed and life was determined
by the presence or absence of breath-fog
ghosting a mirror, bells were placed
in the hands of the newly dead before
their above-ground tombs were sealed.
Then, in case a mistake was made,
some patient awakened from a fever-coma
to find herself accidentally interred could ring
the bell and be rescued. In those days,
a dozen diseases roamed the narrow streets,
calling from each house whoever would answer.
Small wonder those muddy, rutted streets
and abandoned rooms might feel crowded
with spirits bent on unfinished errands. And the watchers
who witnessed the clairvoyant's spirit-conversations
heard all they longed to know and all they feared.
Assured that death is no ending, they were frightened
because the dead must know what we do not,
must roll their blank eyes at the futility
of our scurrying. So the bells set
in the steeples of folded hands were a way
to prove the scuffle of this world desirable
and something like triumph must have occurred

in the breasts of those who heard the praise-song
of a bell's metal tongue calling out of the tomb
to the graveyard whistle,
the unresting breath of this world.

For The Players

I would praise the gathering of breath,
that rambling confluence pressed

into the winding of the horn,
the horn's bell lifted to blast

its burnished and untranslatable syllables
into the deafness of waiting air.

I would praise those fingers that feel
their way as fine as a safe cracker's touch

into the instinct that reads how hard
or how easy to go on the notes below them.

Bless especially those who sweat bad sound
out of short-wired amps in half-lit clubs,

playing for audiences wholly lit and earless.
And guide the ones practicing alone

on cheap instruments in small rooms.
Grace the fingers and wind they spend

in thrall to the language of instruments,
ordering tone and breath and time

into the bright math of sound, geometries
of scale and distortion that are the sum

of the solo pounding of our dark red hearts,
arterial drumming we live by,

music that loves us too well to stop.

Night Ride Home

Once we have learned the way back
from anywhere, we begin seeking alternate routes,
trusting direction, believing any road
will finally take us to any other road.
The first miles are reminisce
as we settle on a version of where we have been.
Because we are always coming home in the dark,
our voices are landmarks, assurance
we are taking the right thoroughfare.
Trees in their night robes, somber magistrates,
preside over the road, over the whiskers and blades
of roadside grass that yellow with our approach
and melt black in our wake. Midway, you find the stars,
burning chips of light, while I grip the hollow
our headlights scoop out of the dark before us.
It is now we might sing, two voices
tied in weathered harmony, scatting whatever words
our tongues have not memorized.
 At such times
we might be anywhere, might be any two
of possibility's wayfarers stretched between stations.
And if, in those miles, a deer or raccoon stands
beside the road, yellow eyes lit wth the cold fire
of our passing, it is possible to believe
it might be not simply a beast confused
but your brother or my father, any traveler gone
before us, returning with assurances
that the road leads exactly where we need it to.
So in the last miles, before all becomes familiar,
gravity-defined once more, we will be silent,
passengered by those who will not ride with us again,
who have left us to the careening
of this larger vehicle we all ride
to the familiar and unlit destination
we will not call home.

About the Author

Al Maginnes was born in Quincy, Massachusetts in 1957 and grew up in a number of states, mostly in the southeast. He has degrees from East Carolina University and the University of Arkansas. Currently he teaches at Wake Technical Community College in Raleigh, North Carolina, where he lives with his wife, Jamie.